KENT

Alan Kay is a retired school master who has lived and worked in Kent all his life, and has written many books and articles on the county's unrivalled heritage.

PHOTOGRAPHIC MEMORIES
OF BRITAIN

PHOTOGRAPHIC MEMORIES OF BRITAIN
KENT

ALAN KAY

First published in the United Kingdom in 2003 by
Frith Book Company Ltd

Hardback Edition 2003
ISBN 1-85937-768-8

British Library Cataloguing in Publication Data

Photographic Memories of Britain - Kent
Alan Kay

Frith Book Company Ltd
Frith's Barn, Teffont,
Salisbury, Wiltshire SP3 5QP
Tel: +44 (0) 1722 716 376
Email: info@francisfrith.co.uk
www.francisfrith.co.uk

Printed and bound in Great Britain

Front Cover: **BROADSTAIRS,** *The Beach 1907* 58327
Frontispiece: **ROCHESTER,** *The Castle and the Cathedral 1894* 34029

AS WITH ANY HISTORICAL DATABASE THE FRITH ARCHIVE IS CONSTANTLY
BEING CORRECTED AND IMPROVED AND THE PUBLISHERS WOULD
WELCOME INFORMATION ON OMISSIONS OR INACCURACIES

CONTENTS

FRANCIS FRITH
VICTORIAN PIONEER

FRANCIS FRITH, founder of the world-famous photographic archive, was a complex and multi-talented man. A devout Quaker and a highly successful Victorian businessman, he was philosophic by nature and pioneering in outlook.

By 1855 he had already established a wholesale grocery business in Liverpool, and sold it for the astonishing sum of £200,000, which is the equivalent today of over £15,000,000. Now a very rich man, he was able to indulge his passion for travel. As a child he had pored over travel books written by early explorers, and his fancy and imagination had been stirred by family holidays to the sublime mountain regions of Wales and Scotland. 'What lands of spirit-stirring and enriching scenes and places!' he had written. He was to return to these scenes of grandeur in later years to 'recapture the thousands of vivid and tender memories', but with a different purpose. Now in his thirties, and captivated by the new science of photography, Frith set out on a series of pioneering journeys up the Nile and to the Near East that occupied him from 1856 until 1860.

INTRIGUE AND EXPLORATION

These far-flung journeys were packed with intrigue and adventure. In his life story, written when he was sixty-three, Frith tells of being held captive by bandits, and of fighting 'an awful midnight battle to the very point of surrender with a deadly pack of hungry, wild dogs'. Wearing flowing Arab costume, Frith arrived at Akaba by camel seventy years before Lawrence of Arabia, where he encountered 'desert princes and rival sheikhs, blazing with jewel-hilted swords'.

He was the first photographer to venture beyond the sixth cataract of the Nile. Africa was still the mysterious 'Dark Continent', and Stanley and Livingstone's historic meeting was a decade into the future. The conditions for picture taking confound belief. He laboured for hours in his wicker dark-room in the sweltering heat of the desert, while the volatile chemicals fizzed dangerously in their trays. Back in London he exhibited his photographs and was 'rapturously cheered' by members of the Royal Society. His reputation as a photographer was made overnight.

VENTURE OF A LIFE-TIME

Characteristically, Frith quickly spotted the opportunity to create a new business as a specialist publisher of photographs. He lived in an era of immense and sometimes violent change.

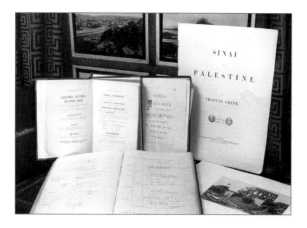

For the poor in the early part of Victoria's reign work was exhausting and the hours long, and people had precious little free time to enjoy themselves. Most had no transport other than a cart or gig at their disposal, and rarely travelled far beyond the boundaries of their own town or village. However, by the 1870s the railways had threaded their way across the country, and Bank Holidays and half-day Saturdays had been made obligatory by Act of Parliament. All of a sudden the working man and his family were able to enjoy days out and see a little more of the world.

With typical business acumen, Francis Frith foresaw that these new tourists would enjoy having souvenirs to commemorate their days out. In 1860 he married Mary Ann Rosling and set out on a new career: his aim was to photograph every city, town and village in Britain. For the next thirty years he travelled the country by train and by pony and trap, producing fine photographs of seaside resorts and beauty spots that were keenly bought by millions of Victorians. These prints were painstakingly pasted into family albums and pored over during the dark nights of winter, rekindling precious memories of summer excursions.

THE RISE OF FRITH & CO

Frith's studio was soon supplying retail shops all over the country. To meet the demand he gath-

ered about him a small team of photographers, and published the work of independent artist-photographers of the calibre of Roger Fenton and Francis Bedford. In order to gain some understanding of the scale of Frith's business one only has to look at the catalogue issued by Frith & Co in 1886: it runs to some 670 pages, listing not only many thousands of views of the British Isles but also many photographs of most European countries, and China, Japan, the USA and Canada - note the sample page shown on page 9 from the hand-written Frith & Co ledgers recording the pictures. By 1890 Frith had created the greatest specialist photographic publishing company in the world, with over 2,000 sales outlets - more than the combined number that Boots and WH Smith have today! The picture on the next page shows the Frith & Co display board at Ingleton in the Yorkshire Dales (left of window). Beautifully constructed with a mahogany frame and gilt inserts, it could display up to a dozen local scenes.

POSTCARD BONANZA

The ever-popular holiday postcard we know today took many years to develop. In 1870 the Post Office issued the first plain cards, with a pre-printed stamp on one face. In 1894 they allowed other publishers' cards to be sent through the mail with an attached adhesive half-penny stamp. Demand grew rapidly, and in 1895 a new size of postcard was permitted called the court card, but there was little room for illustration. In 1899, a year after Frith's death, a new card measuring 5.5 x 3.5 inches became the standard format, but it was not until 1902 that the divided back came into being, so that the address and message could be on one face and a full-size illustration on the other. Frith & Co were in the vanguard of postcard development: Frith's sons Eustace and Cyril continued their father's monumental task, expanding the number of views offered to the public and recording more

5	.	*St Catherine's College*			+			
6	.	*Senate House & Library*		+				
7	.			+				
8	.				+			
9	.	*Gerrard Hostel Bridge*		+	+	+	+	
3 0	.	*Geological Museum*			+			
1	.	*Addenbrooke's Hospital*			+			
2	.	*St Mary's Church*			+			
3	.	*Fitzwilliam Museum, Pitt Press &c*			+			
4	.				+			
5		*Buxton, The Crescent*				+		
6		*The Colonnade*				+		
7		*Public Gardens*				+		
8						+		
9		*Haddon Hall, View from the Terrace*				+		
4 0		*Miller's Dale*				+		

and more places in Britain, as the coasts and countryside were opened up to mass travel.

Francis Frith had died in 1898 at his villa in Cannes, his great project still growing. The archive he created continued in business for another seventy years. By 1970 it contained over a third of a million pictures showing 7,000 British towns and villages.

FRANCIS FRITH'S LEGACY

Frith's legacy to us today is of immense significance and value, for the magnificent archive of evocative photographs he created provides a unique record of change in the cities, towns and villages throughout Britain over a century and more. Frith and his fellow studio photographers revisited locations many times down the years to update their views, compiling for us an enthralling and colourful pageant of British life and character.

We are fortunate that Frith was dedicated to recording the minutiae of everyday life. For it is this sheer wealth of visual data, the painstaking chronicle of changes in dress, transport, street layouts, buildings, housing, engineering and landscape that captivates us so much today. His remarkable images offer us a powerful link with the past and with the lives of our ancestors.

THE VALUE OF THE ARCHIVE TODAY

Computers have now made it possible for Frith's many thousands of images to be accessed almost instantly. Frith's images are increasingly used as visual resources, by social historians, by researchers into genealogy and ancestry, by architects and town planners, and by teachers involved in local history projects.

In addition, the archive offers every one of us an opportunity to examine the places where we and our families have lived and worked down the years. Highly successful in Frith's own era, the archive is now, a century and more on, entering a new phase of popularity. Historians consider the Francis Frith Collection to be of prime national importance. It is the only archive of its kind remaining in private ownership. Francis Frith's archive is now housed in an historic timber barn in the beautiful village of Teffont in Wiltshire. Its founder would not recognize the archive office as it is today. In place of the many thousands of dusty boxes containing glass plate negatives and an all-pervading odour of photographic chemicals, there are now ranks of computer screens. He would be amazed to watch his images travelling round the world at unimaginable speeds through internet lines.

The archive's future is both bright and exciting. Francis Frith, with his unshakeable belief in making photographs available to the greatest number of people, would undoubtedly approve of what is being done today with his lifetime's work. His photographs depicting our shared past are now bringing pleasure and enlightenment to millions around the world a century and more after his death.

The archive's future is both bright and exciting.

KENT
AN INTRODUCTION

KENT ranks ninth in size among the counties of England, and perhaps no county has more history within its boundaries than Kent. Separated from Europe by only 21 miles of sea, it has been invaded by foreign powers over the centuries. It also has been the target for several failed invasions, from the time of the Napoleonic Wars in the 19th century, to 1940, when Hitler's invasion plans envisaged landing on the Kent coast.

Kent's main significance is that it is the nearest county to the continent, and lies between it and London. Deal and Dover are closer to France than they are to Maidstone. This unique geographical position, as a natural corridor between London and France, has caused Kent both to benefit and to suffer. The 'White Cliffs of Dover' have always provided a welcome to travellers returning to England, from holidaymakers in

AYLESFORD, *The Village and Bridge c1960* A85017

peacetime, to armed services personnel during times of trouble.

Julius Caesar and his Roman legions penetrated into Kent in 54-55 BC; the local tribesmen were the Cantiaci, from whom Kent gets its name - thus Kent is probably the oldest county name in Britain. Kent became part of the Roman Empire for the next 400 years, and then became the first Saxon kingdom when King Ethelbert became King of Kent and compiled the earliest code of English law and justice, the basis of our legal system today.

This book is obviously not the place to detail Kent's involvement in matters of national importance over the next 1500 years of our history. It is enough to say that its proximity to Europe has always made it our front line of defence against invasions through the centuries. Even today, Kent is the magnet for thousands of unfortunate people endeavouring to cross the Channel to escape persecution in their own lands and hoping to make a better life for themselves.

Twice during the 20th century Kent has been on the edge of a battlefield. In the First World War hundreds of thousands of soldiers left our Channel ports to their deaths during the four years of horror in the trenches of the Western Front. Twenty years later, with the rise of Hitler, Kent welcomed refugees from Nazism. Later, the full impact of the Second World War was felt in

AYLESFORD, *Kits Coty House 1898* 41555
Kits Coty House is all that remains of what was an impressive entrance chamber to a Neolithic long barrow. It is said that this ancient monument takes its name from a local shepherd named Kit, who used these stones as a shelter in the 17th century.

May 1940, when a fleet of small ships evacuated a large part of the British army from the beaches of Dunkirk. Defences against a possible invasion of Kent were made, pillboxes and barbed wire barriers were prepared, and many civilians and schoolchildren were evacuated from Kent towns. The Battle of Britain was fought over the county in 1940. During the Second World War over 3000 civilians in Kent were killed by bombs, flying bombs, rockets and even shelling from the French coast.

This book is dependent to a great extent on what is available from the Francis Frith Archive, which contains photographs taken only up to the late 1960s. However, it would be remiss to omit references to the great changes in transport which have occurred over the past forty years. So to introduce the 21st century scenes are included from the Channel Tunnel Terminal at Folkestone and the great expansion of the ferry facilities at Dover for passengers and freight.

I hope this collection of scenes and captions showing Kent from around 1890 into the 21st century will encourage many who do not know Kent very well to visit its attractions in greater detail, and not just to rush through the county on the motorways to the ferry ports or on the Eurostar through the Channel Tunnel. This 'Gateway to England' deserves much better.

FOLKESTONE, *The M20 Motorway 2003* F35701

The motorway system has changed the road patterns over most of the county of Kent. The M20 and the M2 have bypassed small villages and larger towns and provided speedy links between the ferry and rail terminals on the Channel and London and beyond. Thousands of cars take holidaymakers in search of the sun and leisure, while daily streams of articulated lorries carry food and imports from all over Europe.

KENTISH CASTLES -
OUR EARLIEST DEFENCES

As we saw in the introduction, the proximity of Kent to Europe has always proved a military liability as well as a commercial asset. Over the centuries large numbers of threatening invaders have marched across the pages of Kentish history. In the 200 years following the Norman Conquest eleven castles were built in Kent, mostly by local lords to defend strategic points. Not only were they built to defend against external invasions, but many were built to enforce law and order. Castles at Dover, Rochester and Tonbridge all figured in struggles between kings and barons. Today some are in ruins.

OTFORD, *The Palace Ruins c1950* O87008

At the battle of Otford in about 776, the Kentish men fought against Offa, king of Mercia. Otford Palace was one of the residences of the Archbishop of Canterbury from the 9th century; in the early 16th century, Archbishop Warham rebuilt the palace - it used to be as large and grand as Hampton Court, but today only part of the gatehouse remains.

ROCHESTER
The Castle and the Cathedral 1894 34029

This fine example of a Norman castle was built by William the Conqueror (1080-1126) in a strategic position to control the crossing point over the Medway. The castle has walls 20ft thick; the stone keep was added in 1127, the highest in the country. After several sieges the castle declined in importance, and only narrowly escaped total demolition in the 18th century. During the Roman period, Rochester controlled Watling Street, the Roman road to London.

◄ **SALTWOOD**
The Castle 1890 25896

The impressive 14th-century twin watch towers and the stone curtain walls we see here are still the main feature today. The knights who killed Thomas a Beckett used Saltwood as their base from which to plan the horrendous murder in Canterbury Cathedral. The castle was the home of Kenneth Clarke, the art historian, and then of his son Alan Clarke, the politician and diarist. It is open during the summer, when the 13th-century crypt, the dungeons and the armoury can be seen.

◄ DOVER
The Castle 1890 25709

Dover Castle is possibly the most impressive of castles in Kent, perched loftily on the cliffs overlooking the harbour, symbolic of the defence of our nation against every threat of invasion over the past 950 years. The massive stone-walled keep in the centre was begun by the Normans in 1180, but there has been a fortified stronghold here since the Romans. Dover Castle was severely tested in the Civil Wars of the 17th century, when Kent was as passionately split as the rest of the country.

◄ DEAL
The Castle 1924 76073

Henry VIII regarded the Kent coastline here as particularly vulnerable. He strengthened his defences with a castle in the shape of a Tudor rose, with gun emplacements facing in all directions. Deal and nearby Walmer were members of the Cinque Ports, and their castles were important to the nation's defence during the Middle Ages.

▼ LEEDS CASTLE *1898* 41568

Leeds Castle is near Maidstone, and is said to be 'the loveliest castle in the world'. It was first built by a Norman baron; it became the home of six medieval kings before becoming the romantic strongholds of private landowners, particularly the Culpeppers and the Fairfaxes, who played major roles in settling our colonies. It was purchased by the Hon Lady Olive Baillie in 1926, and it was left to the nation when she died in 1974.

▼ KINGSGATE, *The Castle c1965* K124041

Despite its name, Kingsgate Castle has never featured in any defence of our nation. From 1760 onwards, a series of follies were erected at Kingsgate by Lord Holland, Charles Fox's father. One of the first was Holland House, a mansion overlooking the bay. The original stabling and servants' quarters on the cliff edge were later extended and enlarged in the 19th century into the present building with its square turrets and battlements, and became a private house for several wealthy aristocrats. Between the wars it became a luxury hotel, and after the Second World War it was converted into maisonettes.

▲ CHIDDINGSTONE
The Castle and the Lake c1955 C86018

This is another 'castle' which is a sham. From the 14th century onwards, the estate was owned by the Cobham, Burghest and Streatfield families, who lived in the manor house. Towers, turrets and battlements were added in 1889, so that the house gave the appearance of being a castle. The estate now belongs to the National Trust.

◄ MAIDSTONE
Allington Castle 1898 41546

Allington Castle is best viewed from the towpath on a bend of the Medway near Maidstone. It was built at the end of the 15th century, and was the home of Sir Henry Wyatt, a member of a well-known Kentish land-owning family. With the downfall of the Wyatts in the 16th century, years of decay and neglect took their toll. Seriously damaged by fire, the ruins were bought by Lord Conway in 1905, who spent a fortune and a quarter of a century in restoration work. All that now remains of the original fabric is a great tithe barn and the impressive arch of a gatehouse. The castle is now a retreat home of the Carmelite Friary.

19

CANTERBURY
The Cathedral, North Side 1890 25671

This magnificent cathedral is still a magnet for countless tourists from all over the world. The tall Bell Harry tower (built between 1494 and 1503) is a landmark for miles in an otherwise flat landscape. To the left of the Bell Harry Tower is the 12th-century choir and to the right the glorious Perpendicular nave, begun in 1378 and completed in 1410. The nave then ends in the lesser south-west towers. The cathedral is still used as a daily place of worship, and despite many air raids on Canterbury during the Second World War, it remains relatively undamaged.

RELIGION AND KENT

THE EARLIEST religious communities arose in Kent after King Ethelbert welcomed St Augustine and his 40 monks near Ebbsfleet (Pegwell Bay) in 597. This began over 500 years of conversion to Christianity and the growth and development of the church in the county. Canterbury's primacy in church affairs was partly caused by its acquisition of many wealthy land-owning estates. It became the cradle of English Christianity, with the Archbishop of Canterbury an important figure in the English constitution. Canterbury later became the great centre for pilgrimage as a result of the murder of Thomas a Beckett in the cathedral; Thomas's subsequent beatification belongs both to the history and religion of our country.

Religion was a major motivation in men's lives through the 11th and 12th centuries, when so many Norman churches in Kent were built. The ancient parish churches of most Kentish villages often give character to the whole village. The church had a profound influence, not only on men's souls, but on the landscape - the church towers are striking landmarks. Norman architecture is common in most Kentish parish churches, which are often the oldest buildings in the village. Frith's photographs carry us from the 21st century to a bygone age, but in all villages the church still occupies an important part in the life of the community.

CANTERBURY, *Christchurch Gate c1860* 329

This magnificent intricately carved entrance (1517) leads into the cathedral close. The cathedral was originally founded in 598 for the monks of St Augustine, and it was later embellished in the 15th century, when the fame of the shrine of Thomas à Beckett spread to every corner of the Christian world. This led to the cathedral becoming the focus for pilgrimages.

ROCHESTER, *The Cathedral from the Castle 1894* 34013

This cathedral is a modest one: it is only 310ft in length, with a fairly squat tower. King Ethelbert built the first church here in 604, soon after he was converted to Christianity. Later a choir was added in 1227, ushering in the Early English style of architecture. The nave is a fairly plain rectangular box, appearing harsh and gaunt compared with the glory of Canterbury.

23

AYLESFORD, *The Village and Bridge c1960* A85017

This well-known view of the church also shows the medieval Kentish ragstone bridge and red tiled roofs and gables overlooking the Medway. A Carmelite friary was founded here in 1242 by some monks from the Holy Land, but the community closed after Henry VIII's Dissolution of the Monasteries in the 1530's. The religious connection was re-established in 1949, after four hundred years of private ownership. Many of the old buildings are much restored, thus linking the old order with the new, although some were affected by the disastrous floods of 1965.

BILSINGTON
The Priory 1909 61579

During the 13th century, many great landowners were prepared to devote part of their wealth to the establishment of monastic houses. From 1253 onwards, Bilsington Priory was used as lodgings by the Archbishops of Canterbury on their periodic visits to Romney Marsh. At that time the site was near the sea coast, but now, through land deposition, it is four miles from the sea. Through the centuries this priory became a spiritual and physical retreat from the cares of the world.

CHILHAM, *The Church 1925* 77015

Isolated from through traffic, Chilham has one of the prettiest squares in Kent, which lies between the churchyard of St Mary's church and the entrance gates to Chilham Castle, set in its park of 300 acres. This church is built of Kentish ragstone, with the fine tower of Caen stone and flint. The White Horse flanks the church entrance, a favourite resting place through the centuries for Canterbury pilgrims. The inn dates from the 15th century, and was the alehouse used for festivals held in the parish church.

CHARING
The Church c1955 C60001

Charing lies at a junction of ancient roads, and was another stopping place for the pilgrims. The manor of Charing was held by the Archbishop of Canterbury. The building alongside the church was often known as 'the palace'; Henry VIII stayed here before meeting Francis I of France on the Field of the Cloth of Gold. The crumbled remains of a medieval farmhouse stand to the left of the parish church - the old barn has now been converted into the village hall.

◄ APPLEDORE
The Church c1955
A231005

This pleasant 13th-century church is of several periods, and was severely restored in the 19th century. It is situated on the road from Hythe to Rye, perched above the Royal Military Canal. This canal behind the church is a reminder of Napoleon's threatened invasion of Kent, and runs 30 miles from Hythe nearly as far as Hastings.

◄ CHARTHAM
The Church and Green
1903 50354

Another old-established village parish church is at Chartham, again on the pilgrims' route to Canterbury. St Mary's church introduced the Decorated style of church architecture to Kent at the end of the 13th century. The church appears relatively plain, but the large windows with their delicate tracery have been restored. The village, down the lane, possesses one of the 25 watermills on the Great Stour.

ASH
The Village c1965 A232029

The church tower of St Nicholas was built in the late 15th century. The tall leaded needle spire was added in the 18th century as a navigation aid to shipping, and is kept in repair by Trinity house. This parish church contains many impressive brasses and monuments. Ash is the centre for the vegetable and potato farming in East Kent.

◄ EASTRY
Church Lane c1955
E154016

The church at Eastry, near Sandwich, is dedicated to St Mary the Virgin. It was built in the early 13th century of Caen stone and flint, but is now very much restored. The square tower leads into an impressive nave with five bays of 1230.

OUR RURAL PAST

Until the early 19th century, settlement in Kent was mainly rural in small communities. In 1821 only one fifth of the county's population lived in one of the main twelve towns, thus the past has bequeathed a rural landscape of independent farmsteads, hamlets and rural villages. As the century progressed, many improvements have been made to village housing and services; but increasingly the younger generations of rural folk have had to find work in, and commute to, the nearest large town. Although much agricultural land in Kent is under the plough, there are still areas of orchards, and also of hop gardens and their associated oast houses, so typical of the country landscape of the past. Hops were first introduced by Flemish weavers in the 16th century. In the days when beer was a staple drink for the working classes, there was a great demand for hops from the brewers.

CRANBROOK
The Village 1908 60289

Kent's countryside was a simple, uncomplicated landscape of fields, with hedgerows full of wildlife. Agriculture and its ancillary trades were the principal sources of village employment, with the farmyard at its heart.

▼ WESTERHAM, *West Way 1925* 78201

This, the westernmost town in Kent, stands at the source of the River Darent in the midst of cleared woodland. A compact town of old houses, antique shops, pubs and tea rooms, it is now freed from earlier traffic congestion by the M25 motorway. Westerham has associations with two famous men, General Wolfe at Quebec House, and Winston Churchill who built Chartwell.

▶ RAMSGATE
The Old Mill 1901 48045

Most communities would have had a windmill for grinding corn for the local bakers, but the majority have now disappeared from the landscape. This Grange Road mill at Ramsgate was erected in the late 1700s, and was demolished in 1937 after being disused for 45 years. The site is now a parade of shops.

▲ CHARTHAM
A Country Lane 1906 53464

Frith's journeys in the early years of the 20th century took him through a countryside of relative stillness and tranquillity. The motor car had not yet affected our country lanes, and children could still push the family prams in safety.

◀ **CRANBROOK**
Bakers Cross 1901 46444

Up to Victorian times,
cottages were often damp
and cold, and totally lacking
in services. Labourers often
lived in tied cottages. Wages
were low, and did not permit
much spending on
inessentials or luxuries.

▼ **GOUDHURST,** *Mill House 1901* 46395

Now that they are no longer useful, many windmills have been demolished. The Goudhurst mill was taken down in 1890. The old miller's house often remains; this one in Goudhurst has been converted and enlarged into an attractive private home.

▼ **SMARDEN,** *The View from the Church Tower c1955* S533025

Unfortunately, the hop gardens became victims of increasing commercial competition from Europe and the rationalisation of the brewing industry in this country. The familiar landmarks of the white ventilator cowls and wind vanes are disappearing as many oast houses are being converted into private residences.

▲ **GOUDHURST**
Hop Pickers 1904 52570

Hop production was once very labour intensive, particularly when harvesting began on 1 September. With the decline in the rural population, whole families would come down from the East End of London to harvest the bines. This would give them a much-needed income, and also an annual break in the unpolluted countryside. Hop production was once widespread in Kent, but is now located around the Paddock Wood area, with the extensive Whitbread hop farms and the headquarters of the Hop Marketing Board.

◀ **MONKTON**
An Oast House c1960
M257013

After picking, the hops were dried in oast houses - these are typical Kentish examples with their distinctive shape. The hops would be dried for up to 14 hours under controlled conditions to ensnare the famous flavour of English beer. Post-war price cutting and chaotic marketing meant that hop gardens in East Kent, such as Monkton, near Minster, have now given way to housing developments.

THE
VILLAGES

CHILHAM, *Old Houses 1903* 50342

Many feel this is one of Kent's prettiest villages, its square lined with half-timbered Tudor and Jacobean cottages, a church, village stores and the gateway entrance to Chilham Castle. Chilham, straddling the ancient Pilgrim's Way, has seeen the comings and goings of Canterbury Pilgrims for centuries, but is fortunately now bypassed from through traffic.

▲ **PATRIXBOURNE,** *An Old House c1955* P1501   ▼ **HORSMONDEN,** *The Warren 1903* 50555

The Frith Archive is full of village scenes such as these at Patrixbourne and Horsmonden, showing old houses of immense charm. Patrixbourne has a Norman Church from 1170, with a carved stone decorated doorway. Horsmonden is a village of half-timbered and weather-boarded buildings clustering around the Green, known locally as the Heath. The village was a centre of the local iron working industry of the 16th and 17th centuries.

◄ PLATT
The Village c1955
P347045

Platt is another small settlement skirting a long main street, the traffic flow helped in modern times by the building of nearby motorways. The village has a good mixture of old and contemporary buildings, mainly general shops with living accommodation above. Platt is a rare Kentish village, as it does not have a church. The fields around were once a centre of hop growing, now disappeared as a result of economic rationalisation.

EDENBRIDGE
High Street c1955 E21051

Many villages are linear, straddling both sides of a single main street. The long street of Edenbridge is a good example, with fields lying almost at the back door of most of the houses. Several old Tudor weather-boarded and tiled houses line the street, which is now proving much too narrow for present-day traffic. The old Crown Inn, dating from the 15th century, has its signboard spanning the street.

BOROUGH GREEN
The Village c1955 B145008

Borough Green is another community that has been helped by the construction of the M20 motorway. Its proximity to London has created a large commuter development around the station, and the setting up of many light industrial factories has caused it to merge with other communities close by. It was one of the first villages in Kent to have an electric cinema in 1912. Two miles south is Old Soar Manor, a late 13th-century knight's dwelling.

STAPLEHURST
The Village 1903 51071

Staplehurst consists of a ribbon of unplanned cottages on the main Maidstone to Hastings Road. Old timbered cottages flank the raised pavements, with the old-established Lamb Inn in the centre, a stopping-point for travellers over the years.

▼ **LAMBERHURST,** *The Village c1955* L323071

Lamberhurst lies on the Sussex border. It is another linear village, with a long main street edged with weather-boarded cottages. Once a heavily wooded area, Lamberhurst was the centre of old Wealden iron workings, which once provided the railings outside St Paul's Cathedral.

▼ **LITTLEBOURNE,** *The Village 1903* 51053

This charming village between Canterbury and Wingham stands in the heart of pre-war orchard country, now given over to potato production. This lane reflects the sense of rural peace and tranquillity, and stretches back from the main road to Littlebourne's Early English church, an attractive jumble of architectural styles.

▲ **WROTHAM**
The Village c1900 W155301

Wrotham, pronounced 'Root-em', is an old village whose heart has been ripped out by the motorway interchanges nearby. This tranquil 1900 scene could not be recreated today - the village street is now busy with cars and lorries. At its centre the road widens to a small square. Here there is a 13th-century church with a Perpendicular tower on its north side. On Wrotham Hill, overlooking the village, stands an ugly BBC TV aerial, which spoils one of Kent's loveliest vistas.

◄ **LITTLEBOURNE**
The Village 1903
49429

CRANBROOK
The Hill 1913 65426

Some villages expanded by having a local industry. A good example is Cranbrook: Flemish weavers came here in the 14th century, and made the village a centre of medieval cloth making, using wool from the local flocks. The long main street, The Hill, bordered by tile-hung or weather-boarded cottages, turns in the middle, with St Dunstan's church set back above the bend. Cranbrook Mill, in the background, was built in 1814. Restored in 1958, it is regarded as the finest remaining smock mill in the county.

BIDDENDEN, *The Village c1955* B88008

Stone has been quarried in Kent from Roman times for castle, church and house building. Around Biddenden a particularly fine limestone known as Bethersden marble was quarried from medieval times as a help to the maintenance of the notoriously bad roads in Kent. Biddenden is an attractive village, with the wide main street flanked by pavements made of slabs of Bethersden marble. All Saints' church in the centre has a 15th-century church tower also made of the local stone. The church now separates the old village from later modern housing.

ICKHAM, *The Forge and the Street c1960* I1027

Many villages have a history of settlement spanning the centuries, but the staple industry sustaining village life was generally agriculture. Thomas of Ickham built the cemetery gate of St Augustine's, Canterbury in 1390, but Ickham remained a poor corn-producing village with few amenities. Mains water did not arrive until 1913, with gas in 1926 and electricity following in 1931. The old forge has been converted into a garage, and the Duke William Inn, in the centre, is now a private house.

MEOPHAM, *The Green and the Windmill c1965* M253048

Meopham is a sprawling linear village said to be the longest in Kent, an old settlement now engulfed with suburban commuter housing. It did not really develop until piped mains water arrived in 1937. The village green, on the right is the home of one of our oldest cricket clubs, which also gives the name to the Cricketers Inn overlooking the green. The inn dates back to the late 1700s, with a skittle alley and former stables still surviving to the rear. To the left is the splendidly restored smock windmill, first erected in 1801, which still grinds pig and poultry food for the local farmers.

WICKHAMBREAUX, *The Post Office c1955* W92012

This is one of a group of ancient villages a few miles east of Canterbury, typical of Kent's rural beauty before overpopulation took place. It offers a timeless picture of the 13th-century St Andrew's church, a watermill in full working order, a group of timbered cottages, and a Georgian parsonage next to the post office, all encircling a village green.

THE
VILLAGE SHOP

RUCKINGE, *The Village 1909* 61572

A sad result of changes in shopping habits in recent
times has been the loss of the village stores and post
office, the social centre for gossip and community life.
Often the shop would be located in a converted
labourer's cottage, as we see here in Ruckinge, a village
on the ridge overlooking Romney Marsh.

ETCHINGHILL, *The Stores and the Café c1960* E157305

The village shop would often be lit with oil lamps, and would be stocked with sides of bacon, clothes lines and great masses of butter and cheeses for the housewives. Everyday foodstuffs such as fruit, vegetables and eggs were generally produced at home. Often the village stores would double as a café catering for summer visitors, just as we see here at Etchinghill - the cafe is catering for tourists visiting the village and the Royal Military Canal at Bilsington, just a few miles away.

BILSINGTON, *The Canal Bridge 1909* 61580A

◄ **OTFORD**
The Village c1955
O87015

This unspoilt settlement is protected by 'Green Belt' legislation. Otford is sited at a crossing of the River Darent, and has been part of our history for over two thousand years. It was the site of many battles in Saxon and Danish times. Otford Palace was built in 1514. All that now remains is part of the entrance, now converted into cottages of brick facades dressed with stone.

◄ FARNINGHAM
The Village Store c1955
F154001

These general village stores would stock most articles. It would be noticeable that the shop owners dispensed with sophisticated window displays. Village residents do not window shop: they know what they have come in for. Goods not available in the village and luxury items would be delivered by twice-weekly or daily services by the local carriers.

◄ ST MARY'S BAY
The Stores c1960 S538032

St Mary's Bay is little more than a long sea frontage of fine sand with chalk cliffs on either side. Stores such as the one shown here gains custom from sightseers, for the bay is a wonderful spot for watching the incessant and varied shipping passing through the Straits of Dover. The inevitable ribbon development here is protected by a great sea wall.

◄ **PLUCKLEY**
The Village Square
c1955 P57024

As villages expanded, purpose built village stores developed, as shown in this square at Pluckley. An attractive village on a hillside north west of Ashford, Pluckley was the site of an old woollen and weaving industry. The estate was the seat of the Dering family, who suffered financially during the first world war. The black horse insignia is still displayed on the inn sign, and the rounded Dering windows are said to bring good luck to tenants.

◄ **BRABOURNE LEES**
The Village c1955
B578005

The village street at Brabourne Lees has an inn at one end and the church at the other, with the hills of the Downs on one side and the valley on the other. Unlike most Kent villages it has little intrinsic charm, and is not to be confused with the village of Brabourne a couple of miles away, where there was a large military encampment in Napoleonic times.

◄ **SEASALTER**
The Post Office c1955
S524118

Recently, there has been a marked tendency for villagers to patronise out of town retail centres. Understandably, they have provided unwelcome competition, and have led to many closures in rural communities - the shop and post office at Seasalter has now closed.

THE EXPANSION OF THE MARKET TOWNS

SMALL VILLAGES DEVELOPED into market towns, which in turn expanded into many of the Kentish towns we know today. The main change came in mid Victorian times when better communications, particularly the railways, resulted in a predominantly urban population taking over from the mainly rural communities described in the previous pages. The development of the railways in the mid 19th century gave a huge impetus to the towns they served, while the towns missed by the main routes hardly grew at all. The market town of Tenterden was a good example of this. The decay of the old village trades led to the migration from the countryside into the new urban centres.

DARTFORD, *The Mill Pond 1902* 49022

The population of Kent in 1851 was double that of 1801, and was largely caused by the industrialisation of northwest Kent and the Medway towns. These scenes at Dartford at the turn of the century illustrate the change. Here we see the impressive factories and laboratories of the pharmaceutical company Burroughs Wellcome.

DARTFORD, *The Engine Room 1903* 49985

This shows part of the engine room of the Burroughs Wellcome Company, established in 1889, operating later as GlaxoWellcome and now as GlaxoSmithKline. This large pharmaceutical compex on Dartford Creek still preserves, in the modern buildings, some of the early machinery shown here.

TENTERDEN, *High Street 1900* 44993

The long wide High Street is lined with wide grass verges, a relic of the early 18th-century market, now planted with trees. This street has a variety of buildings, some with Georgian mathematical tiles hiding older frontages. St Michael's church with its tower and four large pinnacles dominates the whole area. Built between 1450 and 1500, the tower later carried an Armada warning beacon on the top. The Woolpack Hotel to the right reminds us of the once thriving woollen trade associated with the town.

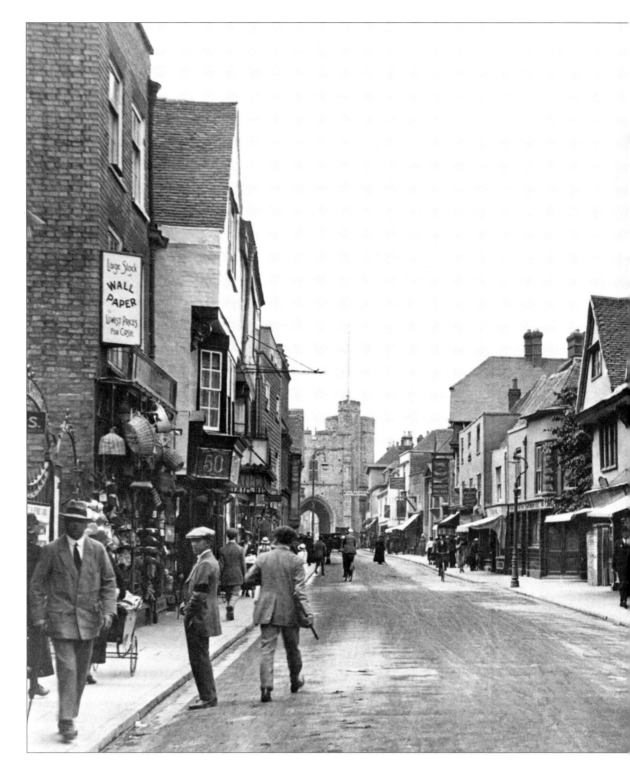

CANTERBURY
High Street 1921 70328

Two hundred years ago, Canterbury was the largest town in Kent with a population of around 6,000. By modern standards its size was minute, but its religious significance to the nation was great. Thanks to modern tourism much of the High Street has been pedestrianised, and the shop fronts shown here modernised. However, the Westgate Towers at the end of the street still retain their medieval ambience.

▼ **CANTERBURY,** *The Weavers' House c1955* C18104

River boat tours for tourists leave from here during the summer season. The pedestrianised High Street is bridged at this point. The Weavers House is shown on the left, a site where the Huguenots and Walloons who fled from religious persecution in the 17th century brought their weaving skills.

▼ **TONBRIDGE,** *High Street 1948* T101003

Being positioned on the main London to Hastings road, Tonbridge has always suffered traffic bottlenecks, even in the supposedly quieter days of horse transport. The original High Street was widened in 1894 to provide for increasing traffic, but some fifty years later the problem still exists.

▲ **TONBRIDGE**
High Street c1890 T1015007

Tonbridge, an old market town, expanded when the arrival of the railway to London in 1868 caused it to double in size, despite regular flooding from the Medway around the town bridge. Apart from the innkeepers who served the through traffic, most people gained their livelihood from serving the needs of the farmers in the weekly markets. Note the sign on the building to the left: 'milk, cream, fresh butter and new laid eggs'. Bordering the High Street is the ancient castle and a great public school. Despite road widening around 1900, Tonbridge still remains a bottleneck for traffic.

◀ **MAIDSTONE** *c1955* M9064

Maidstone owes its importance to its strategic position where the road from London to the coast crosses the River Medway - the bridge across the river is in the centre of the town. An ancient settlement, it was granted its first charter in 1548, and since the early 19th century has been the county town of Kent - most departments of the County Council are here. The early narrow streets of the medieval layout have since been widened to cope with modern traffic. The congestion has now been partly relieved by the motorways by-passing the town.

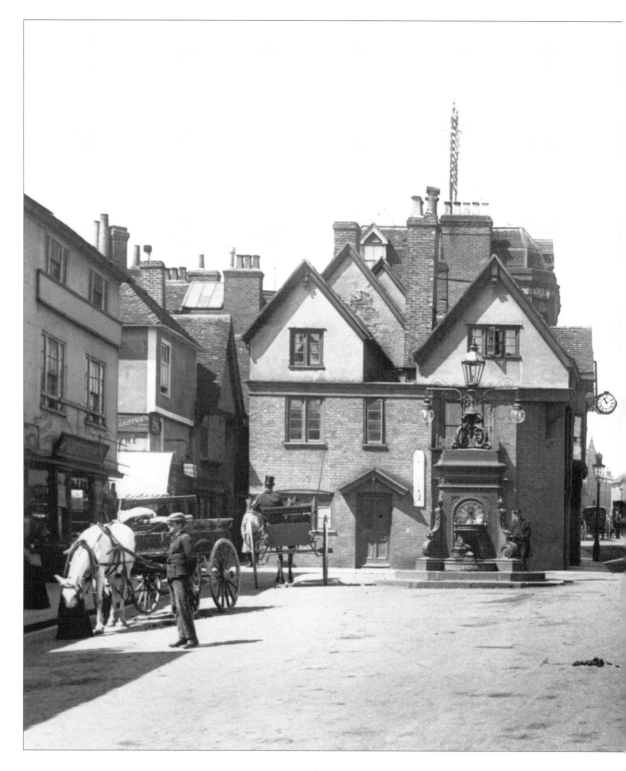

ASHFORD
High Street 1906 53444

In 1801 Ashford's
population was just 2,600.
It was a focus for local
agriculture, with a
flourishing weekly market -
the water fountain and
horse trough (centre) would
provide welcome
refreshment to both horse
and people patronising the
market in front. Ashford's
main expansion came
during the railway boom of
the 19th century, when it
became an important rail
junction. It also became a
centre of engine and rolling
stock manufacture.

ASHFORD, *High Street and the Church 1901* 47524

Architecturally, Ashford's chief interest lies within a few narrow alleyways, enclosing the parish church with its imposing tower. This area is still a warren of gabled shops, overhangs and unexpected corners. Thanks to modern traffic congestion, Ashford has cut a swathe through its town centre with a new inner ring road.

ASHFORD
Bank Street 1903
50331

The width of Bank Street is a reminder of Ashford's role as a market town; roads radiate from here in six directions. Today the town plans to become an important international centre when the Channel Tunnel rail link is finally completed. The M20 motorway, linking London with the Channel ports, has now bypassed the town. Ashford is a growth area, spawning the inevitable housing estates and light industrial factories.

FAVERSHAM, *The Town Hall c1960* F13079

The Town Hall, on stilts, dates from 1574, with the upper storey built in 1814. It stands in Abbey Street, a conservation area, where the 16th-, 17th- and 18th-century timber-framed houses have been imaginatively restored. This part of Faversham had the oldest gunpowder works in the country, supplying the Navy from 1558 to 1934. It also had a small medieval port. It became the centre of England's main fruit producing area when extensive orchards of apples, pear and cherries were planted between the wars to make us independent of foreign supplies. This historic town has now been bypassed by the M2 motorway.

SWANLEY *c1960* S389001

By the early 20th century the sprawling mass of London had spread into the Green Belt of north-west Kent, bringing about the expansion of communities like Swanley. Swanley's increasing industrialisation was helped by the building of the rail junction from London in 1861. The overspill from London meant that Swanley developed into a typically urban suburb, as we see here. Previously it was a major area of glasshouses and flower growing. Now it is an important communication junction on the M25, with motorway links from Swanley to the coast and the continent.

◄ GILLINGHAM
High Street c1960 G226021

Gillingham is now a vast area of depressing urban congestion, with homes for 80,000 people, yet little of note for the visitor. The streets are lined with Victorian terraces, many of them the homes of those who served in the Navy or worked in the dockyard. There are many corner shops and public houses, with the larger shops flanking this High Street. The slopes down to the Medway estuary are now completely built up by the conurbation of Strood, Rochester, Chatham, Gillingham and Rainham, the Medway towns, with a total population of nearly 300,000.

◄ SHEERNESS
High Street c1955 S528034

Sheerness is situated on the northern tip of the Isle of Sheppey, with a long canal to the south which makes it almost an island in itself. The town is in three parts. The High Street (shown here) is Mile Town, the shopping and business centre. East of this is Marine Town, with a seafront and esplanade. The old naval base and dockyard completed in 1665 is known as Blue Town, still out of bounds to all visitors.

▼ TUNBRIDGE WELLS
The Pantiles c1955 T87063

The Pantiles is still a pedestrian precinct; it was built in 1640, with the raised pavement added in 1670, and it still has the atmosphere of a Georgian spa town. Tunbridge Wells became famous after the discovery of the chalybeate spring waters in 1606. The fine Doric columns to the right cover the spring, which was patronised by royalty and nobility who came for their health. In 1698 Princess Anne of Denmark left funds for the paving of the Pantiles. It remained a popular spa through the 18th and 19th centuries, and in 1909 King Edward VII sanctioned the prefix 'Royal' to the town name.

◄ TUNBRIDGE WELLS
The View from Toad Rock c1870 5404

The town still retains an air of charm and tastefulness, with many attractive detached private houses on the outskirts. On rising ground above the town lies the Common. The infertile soils here led to the survival of much uncultivated land. The natural sandstone outcrop of the well-known Toad Rock has been a visitor attraction for nearly 300 years.

COUNTRY HOUSES

THE MOST OBVIOUS symbol of landed power in Kent was the great country house. The owners of the 'big houses' and estates always commanded influence and respect; the land-owning hierarchy of wealthy gentry had had local connections for generations. They were generally patrons of the local church, leaders in rural life, and benefactors of many charities in the villages. Later, the country houses became places of aristocratic resort for leisure and sport. They became the traditional way of life of the English ruling class. Country houses virtually died with the First World War. Estates were sold whole or piecemeal. Many changed hands, as the cost of modernising and the maintenance of the grounds became insupportable. Only the wealthiest of landed proprietors could afford to maintain these large country houses with all that they entailed in servants and upkeep. Newcomers with new money took over the ancestral acres as they became available. The influence of the great country house on village life declined. Many of the properties were converted into training establishments, schools or residential nursing homes.

GROOMBRIDGE *c1960* G216044

The original house was moved in pieces in 1909 to its present site from near Rye. It eventually became a nursing home.

IGHTHAM, *Ightham Mote 1900* 44911

This moated medieval country house, surrounded by woodland, was in continuous private ownership over the generations until it was taken over by the National Trust in 1985. Built in the early 14th century as a fortified manor house, it is possibly one of the finest moated houses in England. It was extensively refurbished in the early 16th century, yet many earlier features remain. This priceless piece of medieval Kent is preserved intact for the 21st century to enjoy.

IGHTHAM, *Ightham Mote, The Stables 1900* 44916

Dame Selby, one of the owners of Ightham Mote in 1605, is said to have been told of the plans for the Gunpowder Plot by a travelling horseman in these stables behind the house. As a result, Guy Fawkes and his conspirators were arrested and executed.

▼ **EASTWELL,** *Eastwell Park c1874* 7089

Eastwell Park was built in 1546, at a time when wealthy landowners were building mansions rather than churches or monasteries. The magnificent gates of Eastwell are still visible, but the house has gone; it was demolished and replaced by a Tudor-style building between the wars. The house we see here was leased to the Duke of Edinburgh, the second son of Queen Victoria, in 1878. His daughter Marie, who later became Queen of Roumania, was born at Eastwell.

▼ **EASTWELL,** *The Church and the Lake 1901* 47539

Eastwell is set in a park of 3,000 acres, three miles from Ashford. The estate has a large artificial lake with a ruined church on the banks. This was damaged by a flying bomb during the war; it finally collapsed in 1951, and its rebuilding was not justified in view of the absence of any estate workers.

▲ **SEVENOAKS**
Knole,
The Lodge Gates c1955
S98001

Knole is one of the largest private houses in Britain with 700 rooms; it stands in an estate of 1,000 acres of parkland. These gates lead into Knole Park, which extends for some nine miles around the house. The building was started in 1457 for the Archbishop of Canterbury -at that time, houses of this great size were built as much for display as for use. Queen Elizabeth later gave it to Sir Thomas Sackville, and today it is still the home of the Sackville-West family, although it now belongs to the National Trust.

◄ **HOTHFIELD**
Hothfield House
1901 47544

Land ownership was the source of much wealth in Kent, and was the basis of the social status of the land-owning families. Profits from farming financed many country houses, but by the late 19th century many were built with wealth made from commerce and land sales, as was the case at Hothfield. The property is now part of the Nature Reserve.

◀ **BEDGEBURY**
Bedgebury Park 1902
48315

This house, on the High Weald, was the family home of the great colonial family the Culpeppers, and was the main attraction of Bedgebury until 1924. In that year the Bedgebury Pinetum was planted in the 2,000 acres of the estate. This national collection of a wide range of conifers was established so that it could escape the polluted atmosphere of Kew. Until recently the building was an educational centre.

◀ **WYE**
Olantigh Towers 1901
47558

This building was financed by the careful estate management of successive generations of the Kempe and Thornhill families at Olantigh, and their investment of rents in the prudent purchase of new estates. The original Olantigh House was built in 1762, but it was severely damaged by fire in 1903 (two years after Frith's photograph). It was rebuilt as a red brick Edwardian mansion with urns and statues in the close-clipped lawns. The imposing portico of Ionic columns survived.

◀ **GOUDHURST**
Pattenden 1901 46388

Pattenden is a fine example of a Wealden timbered, Kentish yeoman's house. Flemish weavers and the wool industry brought prosperity to Goudhurst from the 14th to the 17th century. The house was built about 1470, and was later owned by Henry VIII's standard bearer. Nearby is St Mary's church - it is said that 51 other churches may be seen from St Mary's tower.

◄**PLAXTOL**
Nut Tree Hall 1901
46416

Plaxtol is a hill village. Nut Tree Hall, a pleasant 16th-century timber-framed farmhouse, was renovated in the 18th century. It was built by a wealthy yeoman whose prosperity came from cattle and the local skinneries and tanneries. Adjoining the Hall is a church built in 1649 during the Commonwealth period, an unusual one in that it has never been dedicated to any saint.

◄BENENDEN
Benenden House c1955
B570024

This large, red brick mock-Tudor building, with stone mullioned windows and battlements was built in 1859 for Lord Cranbrook. In 1912 it was bought and modernised by Lord Rothermere. In 1830 Benenden was the earliest village in Kent to have an elementary school, and in 1924 a girls' public school was founded here. It became well-known when Princess Anne was educated at Benenden. The site was earlier known as Hemsted, which superseded an Elizabethan house of the same name.

◄HAWKHURST
Babies Castle 1902
48251

This was originally known as Hall House, and was built in the 17th century when the area was the centre of the Wealden iron industry. Later the building was named Babies Castle, and from here Sir John F W Herschel, as a young man, watched the stars in the night sky. He was the third in a family of famous English astronomers, and was buried in Westminster Abbey.

INNS AND PUBLIC HOUSES

THE VILLAGE INNS of Kent, and the coaching inns, sprang up at strategic points on the main roads leading to London from the coast. The lively, friendly atmosphere encouraged village trade; here farmers, carriers and middlemen would meet to transact business over their beer. Many inns would have paddocks alongside where stock could be kept overnight. The village inn, along with the church and the village school, formed the cornerstone of community life in the village, the focal point of most village activities. It would become the club, almost the home, of the farm labourers in their limited leisure hours. Many farm horses were so accustomed to stop at the wayside pub that they would draw up of their own accord.

HORSMONDEN, *The Gun Hotel 1903* 50554

Originally the Gun was a small inn on the main road, set among hop gardens and woodland. From 1600, this was the site of the Horsmonden charcoal furnace for the local iron ore industry. Originally catering for horse-drawn traffic, the Gun Inn expanded by providing local short-distance coach services to the nearest railway station in 1903. Nowadays the name has changed to the Gun and Spit Roast, advertising the recent restaurant facility at the inn.

RIVERHEAD, *The Amherst Arms Hotel c1955* R319010

This is another example of a recently enlarged village pub. The Amherst Arms Hotel takes its name from Sir Jeffrey Amherst, victor in battles in the Canadian Quebec campaign. Adjoining the pub is a tract of land named Crown Point by Sir Jeffrey - it reminded him of its Canadian counterpart. The inn still carries Sir Jeffrey Amherst's armorial shield on its signboard.

ELHAM, *The Abbot's Fireside c1955* E156023

For many centuries the Abbot's Fireside, a charming black and white timber-framed 15th-century house, has overlooked the wide High Street in Elham. Originally it was called the Smithie's Arms; it was commandeered as the Duke of Wellington's headquarters during the Napoleonic wars. The great door to the left led into the hall of the old inn. The overhanging upper storey housed the great upper room, which was the meeting place for most communal activities in Elham - pronounced 'Eel-am'.

◀ **SMEETH**
The Plough c1955
S534004

Originally, this was known as the Woolpack Inn. The inn's present name comes from the celebrations on Plough Monday, twelve days after Christmas, when ploughs were decorated to raise 'plough money' for a good party for the village farm labourers. Smeeth is a scattered parish of rich farmland; its name means 'smooth clearing', indicating that the plough has always been important here.

◄ HIGH HALDEN
The Chequers c1955 H354003

The Chequers at High Halden, near Tenterden, was first mentioned as early as 1442, and has functioned as a village inn ever since. The brick front hides ancient timber beams, which came from the wrecks of old English galleons. The original fire was in the hall, and a hole in the roof was made for smoke to escape. The tiling here dates from 1650. The interesting inn sign depicts a game of draughts or chequers, said to be the oldest known inn sign.

▼ RIPPLE
The Plough and Portland Terrace c1955 R318009

Another Plough Inn stands in the hamlet of Ripple near Walmer, again showing the importance of local farming. The inn is a typical converted cottage; the traditional spit and sawdust image from the past is now modernised. The ragged hedgerows flanking the lane lead to the churchyard on the right, where Sir John French, Lord Ypres, Commander of the British Army in 1914, is buried - Ripple was his birthplace.

◄ BRASTED
The Stanhope Arms c1955 B580055

The village pump stands on the green opposite the Stanhope Arms. The inn takes its name from Lord Stanhope and his family, who owned the estate and built the imposing premises in 1785.

BRASTED
The White Hart c1955 B580041

The inn sign outside the White Hart has a Battle of Britain squadron badge in the top corner: this was a favourite drinking place for fighter pilots from Biggin Hill airfield during the Second World War. In 1840 it was probably patronised by Napoleon III, who lived in Brasted before his unsuccessful attempt to land at Boulogne and seize the throne of France.

CHIDDINGSTONE, *The Castle Inn c1955* C86016

The Castle Inn stands at the end of the picturesque Tudor High Street with its row of 16th- and 17th-century houses facing the church. This row is now owned by the National Trust, and is often used as a period setting for TV and feature films. Chiddingstone was once an estate village owned by the Streatfield family. In 1780 a sham castle was built to replace the old High Street house on this site. Later, in 1830, the High Street was cut short at this inn and diverted, so that a 3-acre lake could be excavated in the castle grounds.

CHILHAM, *The Woolpack Inn 1913* 65338

The Woolpack lies at the foot of the hill leading into Chilham village, just above the main road from Maidstone to Canterbury. Originally it was a halfway house for smugglers. The green at Chilham was where sheep's fleeces were sold, hence the inn's name. It was once illegal to export wool, so smugglers would ride southwards to the Romney Marsh area to exchange sacks of wool for rum and brandy.

SOUTHBOROUGH
The Hand and Sceptre Hotel 1896 37898

In the 18th century, the Hand and Sceptre was a favourite
night stop for the carriages of the aristocracy travelling to
take the spa waters in Tunbridge Wells - the inn stands on the
main road from London to the inland spa. Facing the hotel is
the village green, where some of the earliest cricket matches
were played, a tradition still continued to the present day.

MINSTER, *Monkton Road c1955* M86001

Monkton Road led to Monkton, or 'Monkstown', part of the extensive estates held by Canterbury Cathedral. Surrounded by fertile fields and pastures, in 1322 the estate carried a 2,000-head flock of sheep. The Freehold Inn to the right had an odd right of way for horses, through the public bar to the stables at the back. Minster and Monkton are now joined along this road by a ribbon development of modern housing.

BROADSTAIRS, *St Peter's 1912* 65029

Now a part of Broadstairs, the farming village of St Peter's was larger than the seaside resort until 1841. The Red Lion Inn on the left, with its open-air tea gardens, was a favourite destination for the horse-brake excursions from the neighbouring seaside resorts. The church in the centre dates from 1070, but the tower was added during the 16th century; it was later used as a warning signal station during the Napoleonic wars.

THE SEASIDE RESORTS

KENT HAS over 126 miles of coastline, with the great advantages of good communications to the large centres of population around London and generally warm, dry summers. The development of the railways in the mid 19th century changed the county; the lines stretched out from London to the nearest stretches of coastline, and in 1851 four of the ten largest seaside resorts in Britain were located in Kent - Margate, Ramsgate, Dover and Gravesend. Broadstairs, Folkestone, Herne Bay and Deal grew in the next few decades.

MARGATE
Donkeys on the Sands 1906 54759

The earliest seaside resort was Margate, popular in the 1730s through its easy, direct access by boat from London. Thanks to cheap rail and paddle-steamer fares in the 19th century, it became a magnet for Cockney day trippers, and Margate acquired an image of vulgarity through their liking for strong drink and their debatable manners.

▼ **MARGATE,** *The Beach and the Bathing Machines 1887* 19689

The original Margate fishing village expanded, and large hotels were built as seaside holidays became popular in Victorian and Edwardian times. In Margate the hotels developed around the jetty and harbour area.

▼ **MARGATE,** *The Hotel Metropole 1892* 31443

This photograph shows a guess-your-weight machine in the foreground - you only paid if the owner did not guess correctly. He made a good living through the clever use of his finger on the weights.

▲ **BROADSTAIRS**
The Beach 1907
58327

The Kent resorts were subject to the class distinctions of the Victorian age. Margate had developed a rather vulgar, working-class image. This allowed Broadstairs to cater predominantly for an affluent middle class. Here we see them enjoying a more genteel and relaxing holiday in their deckchairs.

◄ **BROADSTAIRS**
The Sands 1899
44217

The bathing machines in the centre background assured complete privacy from prying eyes. In 1899 a local by-law forbade any undressing on the beach. Bathing cabins and tents had to be hired, together with voluminous bathing costumes.

▼ **WESTGATE ON SEA,** *St Mildred's Bay 1918* 68422

Another resort catering for the aristocracy and the wealthy middle class was Westgate on Sea, just two miles west of the more popular and unconstrained Margate. Westgate developed as a 'private town' when the railway came through in 1863: prospective residents had to be approved by the owner of the estate. This scene shows many of the detached private residences on the sea front - their plans, again, had to be approved by the owner of the estate.

▼ **FOLKESTONE,** *The Bandstand 1901* 48050

Seaside entertainment was very limited at the turn of the century, and touring military bands playing in the many bandstands offered pleasant relaxation in fine weather. The solid Victorian and Edwardian buildings are a feature of the Leas on the cliff top at Folkestone. The deckchairs would be on the shingle beach, but wooden chairs would be more commonly used on the cliffs.

▲ **DEAL**
The Esplanade
1899 44208

By 1800 Deal was larger than Margate and Folkestone; it also had a bandstand (on the left) and a long promenade fronting the shingle beach, with views of Channel shipping sheltered from the Goodwin Sands. Faintly visible in the background is Deal Pier, famous for its fishing competitions, and one of the last remaining piers on this coast.

◄ **PEGWELL**
*The Seafront and
the Pier c1880*
12739

In Frith's day all
reputable seaside
resorts had to have a
pier, lengthy iron or
wooden structures
stretching into the sea,
used as landing stages
for the steamers and
as stages for varied
seaside
entertainments. All
these piers have now
disappeared, having
succumbed to the
ravages of the seas and
the winter storms.

FOLKESTONE
The Pier 1895 35530

▼ **DOVER,** *Luxury Cruise Liner Berth at Dover 2003* D50701

An additional facility in Dover harbour was opened in 2002 when luxury cruise liners were enabled to berth on their European cruises. Passengers were then taken by coaches on short journeys through the Garden of England to see historic Castles and Cathedrals.

▼ **FOLKESTONE,** *High Street c1955* F35028

The narrow High Street in Folkestone Old Town is still flanked by a jumble of small independent traders, but the main shopping centre has now moved to the Sandgate Road area at the top of the hill.

▲ **CLIFTONVILLE**
The Oval 1918
68436

The Oval, and similar amphitheatres, provided a training ground for many West End and TV artistes who later became famous. This form of entertainment now seems to have died out, as more sophisticated audiences no longer like to sit out in the unpredictable summer weather.

◄ **MARGATE**
*The View on the
Jetty 1887* 19700

89

FOLKESTONE, *The Channel Tunnel Rail Terminal 2003* F35702 (above) & F35703 (below)

The opening of the Eurotunnel Rail Terminal in 1995 wedged between the town and background hills brought a new impetus to the importance of Folkestone. Trains speedily crossed under the Channel in 35 minutes three times an hour in comfort and reliability for passengers and their cars, with special trains for the freight lorries. An added link were the Eurostar expresses linking London (Waterloo) with Paris and Brussels. By September 2003 a fast rail link speeding across Kent approaching 180 mile per hour will provide an additional advantage.

FOLKESTONE, *The Ladies' Bathing Place 1897* 39559

Folkestone developed as a resort when the S E Railway arrived from London in 1843, which also helped the harbour develop as a cross-channel port to Boulogne. The town was generally regarded as a rather superior, exclusive resort for middle-class visitors. This bathing scene illustrates the costume and decorum of the period.

FOLKESTONE, *The Cliff Railway 1912* 64990

As a bathing resort, Folkestone had a shingle beach at sea level, whilst on the cliff top behind was the Leas promenade and extensive lawns. The cliff railway provided a welcome link for the less energetic visitor.

91

SANDGATE
The Cliff Railway 1903
50364

Located westwards from Folkestone and now linked to it as a suburb, Sandgate shared Folkestone's popularity as an Edwardian seaside resort. The cliff railway shown here was built to carry Sandgate's visitors to the attractive cliff top promenade of the Leas. (see the lift at Folkestone on page 91).Henry VIII built a defensive castle at Sandgate using stones from two local abbeys he destroyed. It was strengthened at the time of the Napoleonic War, but was later neglected, and only the remains of the tower have not been washed away by the winter storms.

◄ HERNE BAY
From the Pier 1897
40149

This view was taken from the 3,500ft-long pier, built in 1832 to service the early steamers from London. The clock tower to the left was erected to celebrate Queen Victoria's coronation in 1837, and Herne Bay developed from that period, when speculative entrepreneurs sought to expand this new seaside resort.

◄ WALMER
The Promenade 1906 56928

Adjoining Deal is Walmer, with its medieval castle, the residence of the Warden of the Cinque Ports - an office held for many years by the late Queen Mother. Here on the promenade we see the lifeboat house and its flagpole; the lifeboat is legendary for its rescues of shipping and their crews from the dangerous Goodwin Sands, offshore. To the right is part of the Deal fishing fleet moored on the shingle beach.

▼ HERNE BAY
The Beach 1894 34052

Herne Bay remains a classic seaside resort of the Victorian period, and the design and architecture of many of the buildings and public houses on the sea front around the pier reflect this.

◄ HERNE BAY
The Bandstand 1927
80115

The Victorian bandstand was demolished between the wars, and replaced by the modern layout we see here. The town became popular with commuters after the electrification of the railway to the Medway Towns and London in the 1960s. Estate development also provided homes for a large number of retired people, bringing their pensions and memories.

BISHOPSTONE *c1955* B573008

A noticeable trend during the 20th century was ribbon development on land facing the sea. Bishopstone developed as an eastern extension of Herne Bay, and the frontage here is only a few houses deep. The ground is soft and unstable and subject to sea erosion, which has hindered any real development.

KINGSDOWN, *The Beach 1918* 68509

Kingsdown, between Deal and Dover, is where Kent's celebrated white chalk cliffs begin their march southwards. There has always been sporadic development here, and by 1939 only a few houses and smallholdings had been established, despite land plots being offered at £15 an acre. The sea frontage of shingle has never been developed, and the lack of rail and main road facilities has not helped.

DYMCHURCH, *The Beach 1927* 80400

Another post war development was the establishment of holiday camps along this attractive stretch of coast. The Dymchurch Wall protects rows of holiday homes and prevents the sea from flooding the marshes behind. There has been a sea wall here from Roman times, when the Romney Marshes first started to be reclaimed.

97

THE RIVERS OF KENT

THREE MAIN RIVERS break through the North Downs, all flowing approximately north. The River Medway breaks through a gap at Maidstone on its way to its wide estuary below Rochester. The Stour flows through the Wye valley to Canterbury, and is later joined by two tributaries to meet the sea at Pegwell Bay. The Darent is the smallest of the three; it emerges near Dartford, but it is now much reduced, flowing intermittently through areas dominated by the new motorway complexes.

TONBRIDGE, *The River Medway c1950* T101030

The Medway is only 70 miles long, but has seen a larger span of human history than many longer rivers. In the past it was an important inland waterway: it was navigable by barges as far as Tonbridge after improvements were made in about 1749. The Medway bisects Kent in half. Traditionally Men of Kent are born to the east, while Kentish Men are born to the west of the river.

EAST FARLEIGH, *The Bridge and the River 1898* 41557

The headwaters of the Medway are in the hop garden belt near East Farleigh. Several cowls of oast houses are visible in the centre of this scene. The Medway here is crossed by a fine five-arched bridge built in the 14th century. Below the bridge the flood waters are controlled by a weir and modern sluices.

YALDING, *The River c1960* Y35009

Yalding lies on the Medway flood plain, and the floods of 2000 caused much damage. There is a weir near this narrow 15th-century bridge. In the past Yalding had a small wharf, from which Wealden forest timber was sent down-river to the Navy dockyard at Chatham. From Yalding the Medway valley changes as it is joined by the Teise and Beult waters near Wateringbury.

▼ **LOOSE,** *The Great Ivy Mill 1898* 41563

At Loose, houses hang to the steep sides of the valley. The Great Ivy Mill is just one of the many watermills on this section of the Medway - at one time there were 13 mills in a length of 3 miles. They were established for the early cloth industry here. To the left is the 15th-century Wool House, a reminder of this trade.

▼ **LENHAM,** *High Street c1955* L322002

One branch of the 'gentle Stour' rises at Postling in the Elham valley, while the West Stour rises 17 miles away at Lenham. For most of its course it flows slowly, and it is only really established within a few miles of Canterbury. It was only navigable as far as Fordwich, about 3 miles downstream from Canterbury.

▲ **MAIDSTONE**
*All Saints' Church
c1862* 1481

Maidstone, Kent's county town, owes its prominence to its being an important crossing point on the Medway. One of the best views of Maidstone is from the towpath on the banks of the Medway, where laden barges still come up river from Rochester. All Saints' church dominates the scene, with the Old Palace (the Archbishop's manor house) built in the 14th century to the left.

◀ **GODMERSHAM**
The Bridge 1909
61568

Godmersham is situated in the Stour gap north of Wye. The old bridge of 1698 leads to the great house in Godmersham Park, which is believed to be the original of Jane Austen's Mansfield Park. Behind the building on the right is Jane Austen's 'Bower', a summer house. The flint church near the river is said to have the only statue in existence of Thomas à Beckett.

CHARTHAM, *The Mill on the Stour 1903* 50361

Chartham lies on the old pilgrims' route to Canterbury. This mill is now disused. Many mills such as this were working mills until the early years of the 20th century. There were at least 25 watermills on this section of the Stour, but with the inevitable spread of steam power the mills gradually became silent.

CHARTHAM, *The Riverside 1908* 60304

The riverside at Chartham makes a tranquil picture. The force of the river is quite slow here, giving the river the epithet 'gentle'. The farm labourer's cottage in the centre consisted of just two rooms, a lower hall and a windowed loft above.

CANTERBURY, *The River Stour c1955* C18044

The Stour flows through Canterbury, which was a strategic crossing point over the river in the past. The Westgate Towers on the right form one of the entrances to the city and a defensive point in the city walls.

◄ **STURRY**
The Bridge 1899
44225

The river is tidal at Sturry, which lies a few hundred yards from the medieval port of Fordwich, the farthest point navigable by barges from Sandwich. Fordwich was once the port for Canterbury - Caen stone for the cathedral was landed here. Fordwich was once a limb of the Cinque Port of Sandwich. The bridge now carries the main road from Canterbury to Thanet.

◂ PEGWELL
The Cliffs 1918 68475

The Stour now flows quietly on its final meandering journey from Sandwich to the sea, covering a distance of 12 miles which only takes 4 miles by road. The river reaches the sea at Pegwell Bay, lying between the silted marshlands of the Nature Reserve and the chalk cliffs of the Isle of Thanet.

◂ SANDWICH
The Bridge c1955 S60017

This shows the Barbican Gate; until the recent bypass was built, all vehicles had to pay a toll here to enter the town, one of the five Cinque Ports. In the latter half of the 15th century, Sandwich had 95 ships with 1500 sailors. Deposition and silting from the meandering slow-flowing Stour have left Sandwich two miles from the sea, but it still remains a complete example of a medieval township, despite the encroaching light industrial estates on the outskirts.

SEA AND LAND COMMUNICATIONS

DOVER, *The Castle, the Harbour, and the Ferry Terminal 2003* D50702

With the advantage of its long coastline and partly navigable rivers, only a small part of Kent is more than 20 miles from port facilities. The port of Dover, just 21 miles from the French coast, has always provided a convenient link from Europe to London and beyond. It has featured as a landing point since Roman times, but its importance grew with the building of the railways and the cross-channel ferries between Dover and Calais.

Each year Dover expands its port facilities aided by the growth in individual holidays by private cars and caravans, package tours and group travel. The large roll on roll off luxury ferries make Dover one of Europe's busiest ports. Each year larger and more luxurious ferries are brought into service, with a Cross Channel ferry leaving every twenty minutes during the summer months.

DOVER, *The Car Ferry Terminal c1965* D50068

After the Second World War, with the popularity of private car ownership and with the introduction of package tours and group travel, Dover expanded its port facilities. The large roll-on roll-off ferries made Dover one of Europe's busiest ports.

DOVER, *Cross Channel Ferry Terminal 2003* D50705

Dover increased in importance with the building of the railway in 1850, but the great expansion of the ferry facilities to Calais and Ostend in the late 20th and early 21st centuries has seen the modern terminals taking more and more harbour space each year, resulting in Dover's present position as the world's leading ferry port for passengers, cars and freight.

RAMSGATE, *The Royal Pavilion and the Harbour 1906* 53466

Ramsgate was once a small fishing harbour, but it came into prominence with the building of the great stone harbour in 1749 as a refuge for shipping from the dangers of the Goodwin Sands. In Tudor times Ramsgate had developed links with Ostend and the Baltic, and in the 19th century it became a 'Royal Harbour'. Recently its passenger ferries have faced competition from Dover and the Channel Tunnel, but it still runs freight services.

GRAVESEND, *The Ferry 1902* 49044

Gravesend is another ferry port in decline, mainly through competition from the Queen Elizabeth Bridge and the Dartford Tunnel. Once a busy riverside town giving easy access to London, its importance was at its peak before steam traffic grew in the 1850s. The ferry across to Tilbury and up river to wharves in London's East End was important. Records show that the number of passengers in 1820 exceeded a million a year, and 44 horse-buses would meet the ferries running regularly to the Medway towns and Maidstone. Gravesend was also closely connected with the East India trade: it was the usual practice for ships to take final provisions on board here before starting their long voyages across the oceans.

BRIDGE, *High Street 1903* 49399

The framework for many roads connecting the Channel ports to London, through Canterbury and the Medway towns, was pioneered by the Romans when they built Watling Street some two thousand years ago. The linear village of Bridge lies on the old Watling Street from Dover to London through Canterbury. Today, with the modern motorway system and Channel Tunnel links to Europe, roads give easy access to London and beyond.

WHITSTABLE
The Harbour c1955 W405007

Another medieval port is Whitstable, where the waters of the Swale and Medway meet again after their detour round the Isle of Sheppey; it owes its importance to its position on the coast. Julius Caesar first came here looking for pearls, but the Romans then decided to use the oysters as food. Whitstable Harbour dates from 1832, just two years before the first passenger steam railway ran from Whitstable to Canterbury.

BRIDGE, *Canterbury Hill 1903* 49402

For centuries, Bridge has always been busy, from the days of horse-drawn carriages to the modern articulated lorries from the continent. To the relief of the residents of Georgian houses lining the High Street, the main road was bypassed by the new motorway a few years ago.

BRIDGE, *The motorway between Canterbury and Dover 2003* B199701

A century has passed since these two photographs were taken, and this clearly illustrates the great changes which have occurred to the road patterns over Kent in the last century. Horse traffic in the top photograph has now been replaced by private cars, caravans and articulated lorries.

DUNGENESS, *The Romney, Hythe and Dymchurch Railway c1960* D165010

This small railway opened in 1927; it was used at first to supply the local shingle as track ballast for the national railways. Nowadays these narrow-gauge trains mostly carry holidaymakers, but in 1944 New Romney Station was used to build sections of pipeline laid under the Channel to carry petrol to our forces in France during the war.

ASHFORD, *The Railway Station c1955* A71041

This photograph and F35704 (page 113) illustrate the great expansion in rail facilities which has occurred in Kent over the past fifty years. The Frith photograph of Ashford Railway Station in 1955 is now unrecognisable from the important International Rail Centre complex for the high-speed Eurostar on this site opened in 1995.

FOLKESTONE, *Channel Tunnel Terminal 2003*
F35704

Trains leave for Calais every twenty minutes during the
season, taking just 35 minutes to link Kent with Paris,
Brussels and beyond.

INDEX

Frith Book Co Titles

www.francisfrith.co.uk

The Frith Book Company publishes over 100 new titles each year. A selection of those currently available is listed below. For latest catalogue please contact Frith Book Co.

Town Books 96 pages, approximately 100 photos. **County and Themed Books** 128 pages, approximately 150 photos (unless specified). All titles hardback with laminated case and jacket, except those indicated pb (paperback)

Amersham, Chesham & Rickmansworth (pb)	1-85937-340-2	£9.99	Devon (pb)	1-85937-297-x	£9.99
Andover (pb)	1-85937-292-9	£9.99	Devon Churches (pb)	1-85937-250-3	£9.99
Aylesbury (pb)	1-85937-227-9	£9.99	Dorchester (pb)	1-85937-307-0	£9.99
Barnstaple (pb)	1-85937-300-3	£9.99	Dorset (pb)	1-85937-269-4	£9.99
Basildon Living Memories (pb)	1-85937-515-4	£9.99	Dorset Coast (pb)	1-85937-299-6	£9.99
Bath (pb)	1-85937-419-0	£9.99	Dorset Living Memories (pb)	1-85937-584-7	£9.99
Bedford (pb)	1-85937-205-8	£9.99	Down the Severn (pb)	1-85937-560-x	£9.99
Bedfordshire Living Memories	1-85937-513-8	£14.99	Down The Thames (pb)	1-85937-278-3	£9.99
Belfast (pb)	1-85937-303-8	£9.99	Down the Trent	1-85937-311-9	£14.99
Berkshire (pb)	1-85937-191-4	£9.99	East Anglia (pb)	1-85937-265-1	£9.99
Berkshire Churches	1-85937-170-1	£17.99	East Grinstead (pb)	1-85937-138-8	£9.99
Berkshire Living Memories	1-85937-332-1	£14.99	East London	1-85937-080-2	£14.99
Black Country	1-85937-497-2	£12.99	East Sussex (pb)	1-85937-606-1	£9.99
Blackpool (pb)	1-85937-393-3	£9.99	Eastbourne (pb)	1-85937-399-2	£9.99
Bognor Regis (pb)	1-85937-431-x	£9.99	Edinburgh (pb)	1-85937-193-0	£8.99
Bournemouth (pb)	1-85937-545-6	£9.99	England In The 1880s	1-85937-331-3	£17.99
Bradford (pb)	1-85937-204-x	£9.99	Essex - Second Selection	1-85937-456-5	£14.99
Bridgend (pb)	1-85937-386-0	£7.99	Essex (pb)	1-85937-270-8	£9.99
Bridgwater (pb)	1-85937-305-4	£9.99	Essex Coast	1-85937-342-9	£14.99
Bridport (pb)	1-85937-327-5	£9.99	Essex Living Memories	1-85937-490-5	£14.99
Brighton (pb)	1-85937-192-2	£8.99	Exeter	1-85937-539-1	£9.99
Bristol (pb)	1-85937-264-3	£9.99	Exmoor (pb)	1-85937-608-8	£9.99
British Life A Century Ago (pb)	1-85937-213-9	£9.99	Falmouth (pb)	1-85937-594-4	£9.99
Buckinghamshire (pb)	1-85937-200-7	£9.99	Folkestone (pb)	1-85937-124-8	£9.99
Camberley (pb)	1-85937-222-8	£9.99	Frome (pb)	1-85937-317-8	£9.99
Cambridge (pb)	1-85937-422-0	£9.99	Glamorgan	1-85937-488-3	£14.99
Cambridgeshire (pb)	1-85937-420-4	£9.99	Glasgow (pb)	1-85937-190-6	£9.99
Cambridgeshire Villages	1-85937-523-5	£14.99	Glastonbury (pb)	1-85937-338-0	£7.99
Canals And Waterways (pb)	1-85937-291-0	£9.99	Gloucester (pb)	1-85937-232-5	£9.99
Canterbury Cathedral (pb)	1-85937-179-5	£9.99	Gloucestershire (pb)	1-85937-561-8	£9.99
Cardiff (pb)	1-85937-093-4	£9.99	Great Yarmouth (pb)	1-85937-426-3	£9.99
Carmarthenshire (pb)	1-85937-604-5	£9.99	Greater Manchester (pb)	1-85937-266-x	£9.99
Chelmsford (pb)	1-85937-310-0	£9.99	Guildford (pb)	1-85937-410-7	£9.99
Cheltenham (pb)	1-85937-095-0	£9.99	Hampshire (pb)	1-85937-279-1	£9.99
Cheshire (pb)	1-85937-271-6	£9.99	Harrogate (pb)	1-85937-423-9	£9.99
Chester (pb)	1-85937-382 8	£9.99	Hastings and Bexhill (pb)	1-85937-131-0	£9.99
Chesterfield (pb)	1-85937-378-x	£9.99	Heart of Lancashire (pb)	1-85937-197-3	£9.99
Chichester (pb)	1-85937-228-7	£9.99	Helston (pb)	1-85937-214-7	£9.99
Churches of East Cornwall (pb)	1-85937-249-x	£9.99	Hereford (pb)	1-85937-175-2	£9.99
Churches of Hampshire (pb)	1-85937-207-4	£9.99	Herefordshire (pb)	1-85937-567-7	£9.99
Cinque Ports & Two Ancient Towns	1-85937-492-1	£14.99	Herefordshire Living Memories	1-85937-514-6	£14.99
Colchester (pb)	1-85937-188-4	£8.99	Hertfordshire (pb)	1-85937-247-3	£9.99
Cornwall (pb)	1-85937-229-5	£9.99	Horsham (pb)	1-85937-432-8	£9.99
Cornwall Living Memories	1-85937-248-1	£14.99	Humberside (pb)	1-85937-605-3	£9.99
Cotswolds (pb)	1-85937-230-9	£9.99	Hythe, Romney Marsh, Ashford (pb)	1-85937-256-2	£9.99
Cotswolds Living Memories	1-85937-255-4	£14.99	Ipswich (pb)	1-85937-424-7	£9.99
County Durham (pb)	1-85937-398-4	£9.99	Isle of Man (pb)	1-85937-268-6	£9.99
Croydon Living Memories (pb)	1-85937-162-0	£9.99	Isle of Wight (pb)	1-85937-429-8	£9.99
Cumbria (pb)	1-85937-621-5	£9.99	Isle of Wight Living Memories	1-85937-304-6	£14.99
Derby (pb)	1-85937-367-4	£9.99	Kent (pb)	1-85937-189-2	£9.99
Derbyshire (pb)	1-85937-196-5	£9.99	Kent Living Memories(pb)	1-85937-401-8	£9.99
Derbyshire Living Memories	1-85937-330-5	£14.99	Kings Lynn (pb)	1-85937-334-8	£9.99

Available from your local bookshop or from the publisher

Frith Book Co Titles (continued)

Lake District (pb)	1-85937-275-9	£9.99
Lancashire Living Memories	1-85937-335-6	£14.99
Lancaster, Morecambe, Heysham (pb)	1-85937-233-3	£9.99
Leeds (pb)	1-85937-202-3	£9.99
Leicester (pb)	1-85937-381-x	£9.99
Leicestershire & Rutland Living Memories	1-85937-500-6	£12.99
Leicestershire (pb)	1-85937-185-x	£9.99
Lighthouses	1-85937-257-0	£9.99
Lincoln (pb)	1-85937-380-1	£9.99
Lincolnshire (pb)	1-85937-433-6	£9.99
Liverpool and Merseyside (pb)	1-85937-234-1	£9.99
London (pb)	1-85937-183-3	£9.99
London Living Memories	1-85937-454-9	£14.99
Ludlow (pb)	1-85937-176-0	£9.99
Luton (pb)	1-85937-235-x	£9.99
Maidenhead (pb)	1-85937-339-9	£9.99
Maidstone (pb)	1-85937-391-7	£9.99
Manchester (pb)	1-85937-198-1	£9.99
Marlborough (pb)	1-85937-336-4	£9.99
Middlesex	1-85937-158-2	£14.99
Monmouthshire	1-85937-532-4	£14.99
New Forest (pb)	1-85937-390-9	£9.99
Newark (pb)	1-85937-366-6	£9.99
Newport, Wales (pb)	1-85937-258-9	£9.99
Newquay (pb)	1-85937-421-2	£9.99
Norfolk (pb)	1-85937-195-7	£9.99
Norfolk Broads	1-85937-486-7	£14.99
Norfolk Living Memories (pb)	1-85937-402-6	£9.99
North Buckinghamshire	1-85937-626-6	£14.99
North Devon Living Memories	1-85937-261-9	£14.99
North Hertfordshire	1-85937-547-2	£14.99
North London (pb)	1-85937-403-4	£9.99
North Somerset	1-85937-302-x	£14.99
North Wales (pb)	1-85937-298-8	£9.99
North Yorkshire (pb)	1-85937-236-8	£9.99
Northamptonshire Living Memories	1-85937-529-4	£14.99
Northamptonshire	1-85937-150-7	£14.99
Northumberland Tyne & Wear (pb)	1-85937-281-3	£9.99
Northumberland	1-85937-522-7	£14.99
Norwich (pb)	1-85937-194-9	£8.99
Nottingham (pb)	1-85937-324-0	£9.99
Nottinghamshire (pb)	1-85937-187-6	£9.99
Oxford (pb)	1-85937-411-5	£9.99
Oxfordshire (pb)	1-85937-430-1	£9.99
Oxfordshire Living Memories	1-85937-525-1	£14.99
Paignton (pb)	1-85937-374-7	£7.99
Peak District (pb)	1-85937-280-5	£9.99
Pembrokeshire	1-85937-262-7	£14.99
Penzance (pb)	1-85937-595-2	£9.99
Peterborough (pb)	1-85937-219-8	£9.99
Picturesque Harbours	1-85937-208-2	£14.99
Piers	1-85937-237-6	£17.99
Plymouth (pb)	1-85937-389-5	£9.99
Poole & Sandbanks (pb)	1-85937-251-1	£9.99
Preston (pb)	1-85937-212-0	£9.99
Reading (pb)	1-85937-238-4	£9.99
Redhill to Reigate (pb)	1-85937-596-0	£9.99
Ringwood (pb)	1-85937-384-4	£7.99
Romford (pb)	1-85937-319-4	£9.99
Royal Tunbridge Wells (pb)	1-85937-504-9	£9.99
Salisbury (pb)	1-85937-239-2	£9.99
Scarborough (pb)	1-85937-379-8	£9.99
Sevenoaks and Tonbridge (pb)	1-85937-392-5	£9.99
Sheffield & South Yorks (pb)	1-85937-267-8	£9.99
Sherborne (pb)	1-85937-301-1	£9.99
Shrewsbury (pb)	1-85937-325-9	£9.99
Shropshire (pb)	1-85937-326-7	£9.99
Shropshire Living Memories	1-85937-643-6	£14.99
Somerset	1-85937-153-1	£14.99
South Devon Coast	1-85937-107-8	£14.99
South Devon Living Memories (pb)	1-85937-609-6	£9.99
South East London (pb)	1-85937-263-5	£9.99
South Somerset	1-85937-318-6	£14.99
South Wales	1-85937-519-7	£14.99
Southampton (pb)	1-85937-427-1	£9.99
Southend (pb)	1-85937-313-5	£9.99
Southport (pb)	1-85937-425-5	£9.99
St Albans (pb)	1-85937-341-0	£9.99
St Ives (pb)	1-85937-415-8	£9.99
Stafford Living Memories (pb)	1-85937-503-0	£9.99
Staffordshire (pb)	1-85937-308-9	£9.99
Stourbridge (pb)	1-85937-530-8	£9.99
Stratford upon Avon (pb)	1-85937-388-7	£9.99
Suffolk (pb)	1-85937-221-x	£9.99
Suffolk Coast (pb)	1-85937-610-x	£9.99
Surrey (pb)	1-85937-240-6	£9.99
Surrey Living Memories	1-85937-328-3	£14.99
Sussex (pb)	1-85937-184-1	£9.99
Sutton (pb)	1-85937-337-2	£9.99
Swansea (pb)	1-85937-167-1	£9.99
Taunton (pb)	1-85937-314-3	£9.99
Tees Valley & Cleveland (pb)	1-85937-623-1	£9.99
Teignmouth (pb)	1-85937-370-4	£7.99
Thanet (pb)	1-85937-116-7	£9.99
Tiverton (pb)	1-85937-178-7	£9.99
Torbay (pb)	1-85937-597-9	£9.99
Truro (pb)	1-85937-598-7	£9.99
Victorian & Edwardian Dorset	1-85937-254-6	£14.99
Victorian & Edwardian Kent (pb)	1-85937-624-X	£9.99
Victorian & Edwardian Maritime Album (pb)	1-85937-622-3	£9.99
Victorian and Edwardian Sussex (pb)	1-85937-625-8	£9.99
Villages of Devon (pb)	1-85937-293-7	£9.99
Villages of Kent (pb)	1-85937-294-5	£9.99
Villages of Sussex (pb)	1-85937-295-3	£9.99
Warrington (pb)	1-85937-507-3	£9.99
Warwick (pb)	1-85937-518-9	£9.99
Warwickshire (pb)	1-85937-203-1	£9.99
Welsh Castles (pb)	1-85937-322-4	£9.99
West Midlands (pb)	1-85937-289-9	£9.99
West Sussex (pb)	1-85937-607-x	£9.99
West Yorkshire (pb)	1-85937-201-5	£9.99
Weston Super Mare (pb)	1-85937-306-2	£9.99
Weymouth (pb)	1-85937-209-0	£9.99
Wiltshire (pb)	1-85937-277-5	£9.99
Wiltshire Churches (pb)	1-85937-171-x	£9.99
Wiltshire Living Memories (pb)	1-85937-396-8	£9.99
Winchester (pb)	1-85937-428-x	£9.99
Windsor (pb)	1-85937-333-x	£9.99
Wokingham & Bracknell (pb)	1-85937-329-1	£9.99
Woodbridge (pb)	1-85937-498-0	£9.99
Worcester (pb)	1-85937-165-5	£9.99
Worcestershire Living Memories	1-85937-489-1	£14.99
Worcestershire	1-85937-152-3	£14.99
York (pb)	1-85937-199-x	£9.99
Yorkshire (pb)	1-85937-186-8	£9.99
Yorkshire Coastal Memories	1-85937-506-5	£14.99
Yorkshire Dales	1-85937-502-2	£14.99
Yorkshire Living Memories (pb)	1-85937-397-6	£9.99

See Frith books on the internet at www.francisfrith.co.uk

FRITH PRODUCTS & SERVICES

Francis Frith would doubtless be pleased to know that the pioneering publishing venture he started in 1860 still continues today. Over a hundred and forty years later, The Francis Frith Collection continues in the same innovative tradition and is now one of the foremost publishers of vintage photographs in the world. Some of the current activities include:

Interior Decoration

Today Frith's photographs can be seen framed and as giant wall murals in thousands of pubs, restaurants, hotels, banks, retail stores and other public buildings throughout the country. In every case they enhance the unique local atmosphere of the places they depict and provide reminders of gentler days in an increasingly busy and frenetic world.

Product Promotions

Frith products are used by many major companies to promote the sales of their own products or to reinforce their own history and heritage. Frith promotions have been used by Hovis bread, Courage beers, Scots Porage Oats, Colman's mustard, Cadbury's foods, Mellow Birds coffee, Dunhill pipe tobacco, Guinness, and Bulmer's Cider.

Genealogy and Family History

As the interest in family history and roots grows world-wide, more and more people are turning to Frith's photographs of Great Britain for images of the towns, villages and streets where their ancestors lived; and, of course, photographs of the churches and chapels where their ancestors were christened, married and buried are an essential part of every genealogy tree and family album.

Frith Products

All Frith photographs are available Framed or just as Mounted Prints and Posters (size 23 x 16 inches). These may be ordered from the address below. From time to time other products - Address Books, Calendars, Table Mats, etc - are available.

The Internet

Already fifty thousand Frith photographs can be viewed and purchased on the internet through the Frith websites and a myriad of partner sites.

For more detailed information on Frith companies and products, look at these sites:

www.francisfrith.co.uk
www.francisfrith.com
(for North American visitors)

See the complete list of Frith Books at:

www.francisfrith.co.uk

This web site is regularly updated with the latest list of publications from the Frith Book Company. If you wish to buy books relating to another part of the country that your local bookshop does not stock, you may purchase on-line.

For further information, trade, or author enquiries please contact us at the address below:
The Francis Frith Collection, Frith's Barn, Teffont, Salisbury, Wiltshire, England SP3 5QP.
Tel: +44 (0)1722 716 376 Fax: +44 (0)1722 716 881 Email: sales@francisfrith.co.uk

See Frith books on the internet at www.francisfrith.co.uk

FREE MOUNTED PRINT

Mounted Print
Overall size 14 x 11 inches

Fill in and cut out this voucher and return
it with your remittance for £2.25 (to cover postage and handling). Offer valid for delivery to UK addresses only.

Choose any photograph included in this book.
Your SEPIA print will be A4 in size. It will be mounted in a cream mount with a burgundy rule line (overall size 14 x 11 inches).

Order additional Mounted Prints at HALF PRICE (only £7.49 each*)
If you would like to order more Frith prints from this book, possibly as gifts for friends and family, you can buy them at half price (with no additional postage and handling costs).

Have your Mounted Prints framed
For an extra £14.95 per print* you can have your mounted print(s) framed in an elegant polished wood and gilt moulding, overall size 16 x 13 inches (no additional postage and handling required).

---

* IMPORTANT!

These special prices are only available if you order at the same time as you order your free mounted print. You must use the ORIGINAL VOUCHER on this page (no copies permitted). We can only despatch to one address.

Send completed Voucher form to:
The Francis Frith Collection, Frith's Barn, Teffont, Salisbury, Wiltshire SP3 5QP

CHOOSE ANY IMAGE FROM THIS BOOK

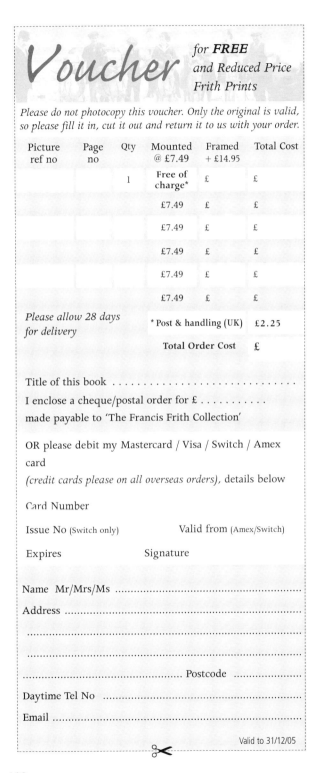

Voucher for **FREE** *and Reduced Price Frith Prints*

Please do not photocopy this voucher. Only the original is valid, so please fill it in, cut it out and return it to us with your order.

Picture ref no	Page no	Qty	Mounted @ £7.49	Framed + £14.95	Total Cost
		1	Free of charge*	£	£
			£7.49	£	£
			£7.49	£	£
			£7.49	£	£
			£7.49	£	£
			£7.49	£	£
Please allow 28 days for delivery			* Post & handling (UK)	£2.25	
			Total Order Cost	£	

Title of this book . . . .

I enclose a cheque/postal order for £ . . . .
made payable to 'The Francis Frith Collection'

OR please debit my Mastercard / Visa / Switch / Amex card
(credit cards please on all overseas orders), details below

Card Number

Issue No (Switch only)   Valid from (Amex/Switch)

Expires   Signature

Name Mr/Mrs/Ms . . . .

Address . . . .

. . . .

. . . .

. . . . Postcode . . . .

Daytime Tel No . . . .

Email . . . .

Valid to 31/12/05

Would you like to find out more about Francis Frith?

We have recently recruited some entertaining speakers who are happy to visit local groups, clubs and societies to give an illustrated talk documenting Frith's travels and photographs. If you are a member of such a group and are interested in hosting a presentation, we would love to hear from you.

Our speakers bring with them a small selection of our local town and county books, together with sample prints. They are happy to take orders. A small proportion of the order value is donated to the group who have hosted the presentation. The talks are therefore an excellent way of fundraising for small groups and societies.

Can you help us with information about any of the Frith photographs in this book?

We are gradually compiling an historical record for each of the photographs in the Frith archive. It is always fascinating to find out the names of the people shown in the pictures, as well as insights into the shops, buildings and other features depicted.

If you recognize anyone in the photographs in this book, or if you have information not already included in the author's caption, do let us know. We would love to hear from you, and will try to publish it in future books or articles.

Our production team

Frith books are produced by a small dedicated team at offices in the converted Grade II listed 18th-century barn at Teffont near Salisbury, illustrated above. Most have worked with the Frith Collection for many years. All have in common one quality: they have a passion for the Frith Collection. The team is constantly expanding, but currently includes:

Jason Buck, John Buck, Douglas Mitchell-Burns, Ruth Butler, Heather Crisp, Isobel Hall, Julian Hight, Peter Horne, James Kinnear, Karen Kinnear, Tina Leary, David Marsh, Sue Molloy, Kate Rotondetto, Dean Scource, Eliza Sackett, Terence Sackett, Sandra Sampson, Adrian Sanders, Sandra Sanger, Julia Skinner, Lewis Taylor, Shelley Tolcher and Lorraine Tuck.